HOW TO DRAW
AWESOME
ANIMALS

HOW TO DRAW
AWESOME
ANIMALS

Author
Susie Hodge

Artist
Steve Roberts

Miles
Kelly

contents

Materials

ALL YOU NEED TO START DRAWING IS A PENCIL AND SOME PAPER, BUT IF YOU COLLECT SOME OTHER MATERIALS AS WELL, YOU WILL BE ABLE TO CREATE EVEN MORE EXCITING EFFECTS IN YOUR DRAWINGS.

Pencils

Soft pencils have the letter 'B' on them and make black, smudgy lines. Hard pencils have the letter 'H' on them, and make light, thin lines.

Soft pencil

Hard pencil

Paper

Try using different papers such as cartridge paper, tissue paper and sugar paper to add extra texture to your drawings.

Buy handmade paper from gift or art shops

Textured papers make excellent backgrounds

Coloured pencils

The simplest way to add colour is with coloured pencils. Some can be blended with water to turn them into watercolours. You can also layer coloured pencils on top of each other to make new colours.

Corrugated paper adds extra depth to bumpy textures

Charcoal and chalk

Charcoal comes in black, brittle sticks, which can be smudged and blended easily to create shadowy, dramatic pictures. Chalk pastels are good for adding highlights, and are best used on coloured paper.

Other equipment

Firm erasers will rub out most pencil and some coloured pencil marks. Kneadable erasers, or putty rubbers, can be squashed into all sorts of shapes to 'lift' marks off the page. A good pencil sharpener is useful. Paintbrushes can be used to add water to water-soluble coloured pencils.

Felt-tip pens

Pens can be used to add a more cartoon-ish feel to your drawings. You can use them to define outlines and create dramatic patterns and markings.

Crayons

Wax crayons can be used on their own or with other materials to produce lots of interesting results.

shading

To HELP MAKE YOUR ANIMAL LOOK MORE SOLID AND THREE-DIMENSIONAL, YOU NEED TO ADD SHADING, OR TONE, TO YOUR DRAWING.

Light and dark

When light shines on something, the parts nearest the light are palest and the parts furthest from the light are darkest. Try to be aware of where the light is falling on whatever you are drawing.

When the light source is below the dog, its front is palest

When the light source is above the dog, its back is palest

IF IT HELPS, IMAGINE THAT THE ANIMAL YOU ARE DRAWING IS SITTING IN THE SUN. WHERE WILL IT FEEL WARM AND WHERE WILL IT FEEL COLD?

How to shade

A shadow always falls in the opposite direction from the source of light. To make your tones darker, add several layers of pencil or charcoal, or use layers of dark colours to build up depth.

Hatching

Using diagonal lines to shade is called hatching. Draw the lines close together for darker areas and further apart for lighter areas.

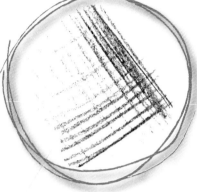

Cross-hatching

For deep shadows add lines across your hatching in the opposite direction to make a criss-cross pattern.

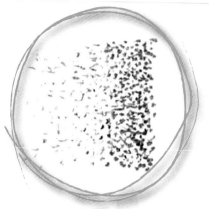

Stippling

Create shading using lots of tiny dots.

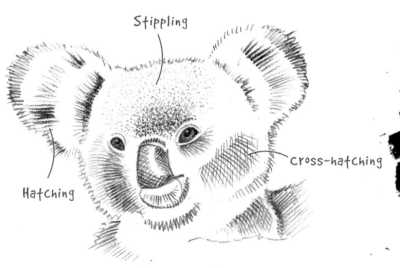

Stippling

Hatching

Cross-hatching

Have a go!

Different ways of shading create different effects. Choose which type suits your animal.

Highlights

The opposite of shade is highlight. This is where the light directly falls, so it's the palest area. Sharp and strongly contrasting highlights can make things look shiny. To make highlights, leave areas of white paper blank, add white pastel or coloured pencil, or 'lift' marks using a kneadable eraser.

Texture

HERE ARE SOME EXAMPLES OF HOW TO MAKE A DRAWING OF AN ANIMAL LOOK THE WAY IT FEELS.

Look and feel

When drawing fur or feathers, start your pencil mark at the base of the hair or feather, pressing quite firmly and lifting your pencil as you move to the end of the line.

Feathers
Use long delicate strokes filled with shorter soft ones.

Smooth skin
Make the dark areas very dark and the light areas very light.

Fur
Draw lots of short lines going in the same direction.

Bumpy skin
Draw lines, squares and circles, pressing quite hard with your pencil.

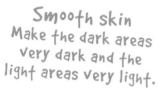

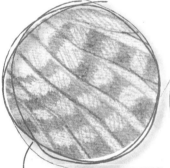

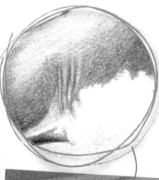

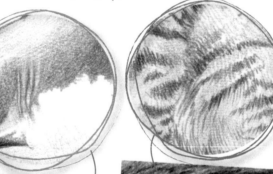

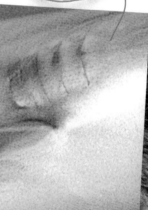

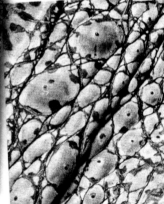

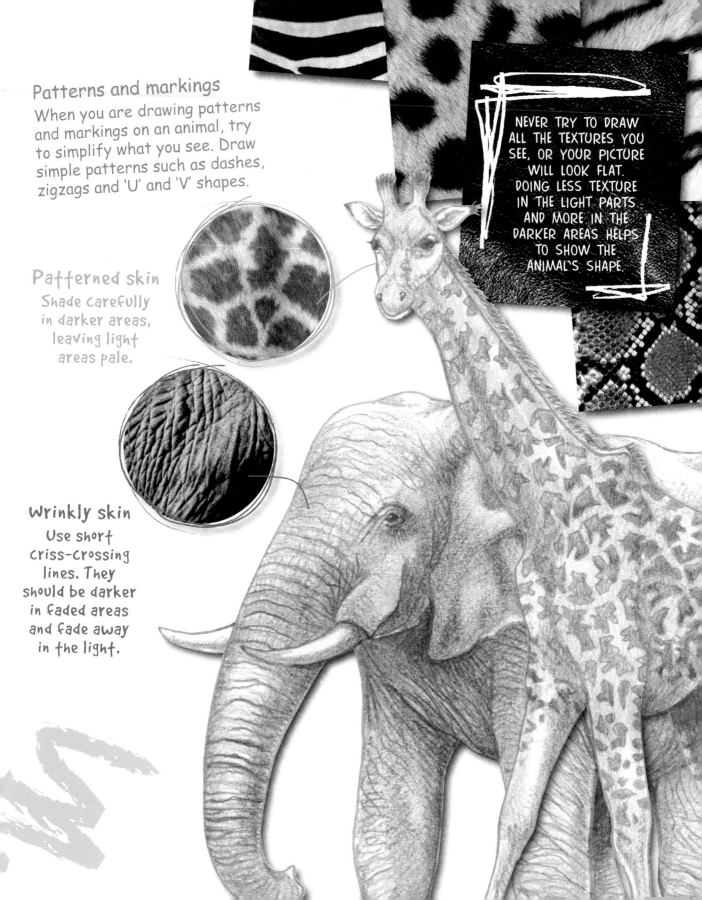

Patterns and markings

When you are drawing patterns and markings on an animal, try to simplify what you see. Draw simple patterns such as dashes, zigzags and 'U' and 'V' shapes.

Patterned skin

Shade carefully in darker areas, leaving light areas pale.

Wrinkly skin

Use short criss-crossing lines. They should be darker in faded areas and fade away in the light.

NEVER TRY TO DRAW ALL THE TEXTURES YOU SEE, OR YOUR PICTURE WILL LOOK FLAT. DOING LESS TEXTURE IN THE LIGHT PARTS AND MORE IN THE DARKER AREAS HELPS TO SHOW THE ANIMAL'S SHAPE.

perspective

OBJECTS THAT ARE FAR AWAY FROM YOU LOOK SMALL, WHILE OBJECTS THAT ARE VERY CLOSE TO YOU LOOK LARGE. SO IF YOU LOOK AT A DOG FROM THE FRONT, ITS NOSE WILL APPEAR MUCH LARGER THAN ITS TAIL.

Big or small

If you are drawing an animal running towards you, its front feet will look bigger than its back feet. From another angle, one ear might seem bigger than the other, or legs that are further away may seem much smaller than legs that are closer to you.

Side View
From the side, most animals look fairly in proportion.

Front View
The tail of this shark appears tiny as it is far away. The mouth and nostrils seem huge because they are close.

Action

AS WELL AS DRAWING ANIMALS STANDING STILL OR SITTING, YOU'LL NEED TO PUT THEM IN MOTION.

Flying owl
This owl is about to swoop, so its wings are outstretched.

Get moving!
Decide which direction your animal is moving in, then sweep your pencil quickly across a piece of paper in the same direction. Use that guideline as the basis for your animal.

Once you have drawn the animal, try smudging chalk pastels or draw broken lines to give the idea of movement.

Running horse
The streaming mane and tail show how fast the horse is moving. The head and neck are extended as the horse lunges forward.

Three legs are off the ground at the same time

13

penguin

1 Draw a long oval for the body and a small oval for the head. Add a triangle for the tail feathers.

3 Draw the eye as a small circle and add a narrow curving beak. Add shape to the wing.

Rub out this line

Wobbly line for the edge of the wing

Little lines indicate soft feathers

2 Add two curved lines to join the head to the body. Draw the legs and feet using short lines.

Draw a pointed shape for the wing

Create the idea of short, smooth feathers with lots of zig-zag lines, keep adding lines to parts you want to be darker.

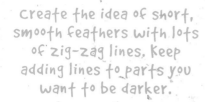

5 Add areas of orangey-yellow around the neck and pale blue to highlight the front.

Patches of dark blue makes these feathers look shiny

4 Shape the toes and claws. Shade in the dark feathers on the back, head, tail and wing.

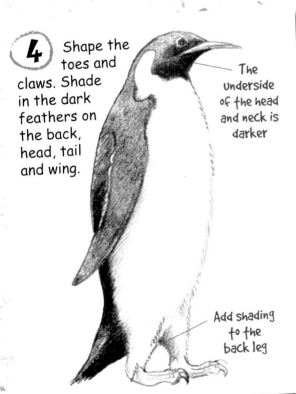

The underside of the head and neck is darker

Add shading to the back leg

Rabbit

1 Draw a fat oval for the body and a smaller oval for the head. Add two thin ovals on top of the head.

2 Draw a large circle for the back leg. Add a small circle for the tail and begin to shape the front leg and the eye, nose and mouth.

Begin to shape the ears

Add curving lines for the neck

3 Use curving lines to link the shapes. Add more shape and detail to the paws and head.

Define the eye

Soften the line of the tail

Add lots of little lines for a furry texture

Use sharp, pointed pencils to draw the fur with tiny lines. The lines should all go roughly the same way.

4 Use different shades of brown to give the fur texture and depth. Leave some areas white.

Frog

1 Draw a large sloping oval with a narrow tip. Draw a squashed oval near the bottom for the front leg. Shape the back leg.

Add a bump for this eye

only part of the back leg can be seen

This eye is a circle with a curvy line above it

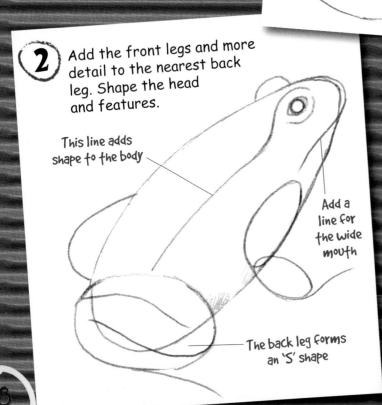

2 Add the front legs and more detail to the nearest back leg. Shape the head and features.

This line adds shape to the body

Add a line for the wide mouth

The back leg forms an 'S' shape

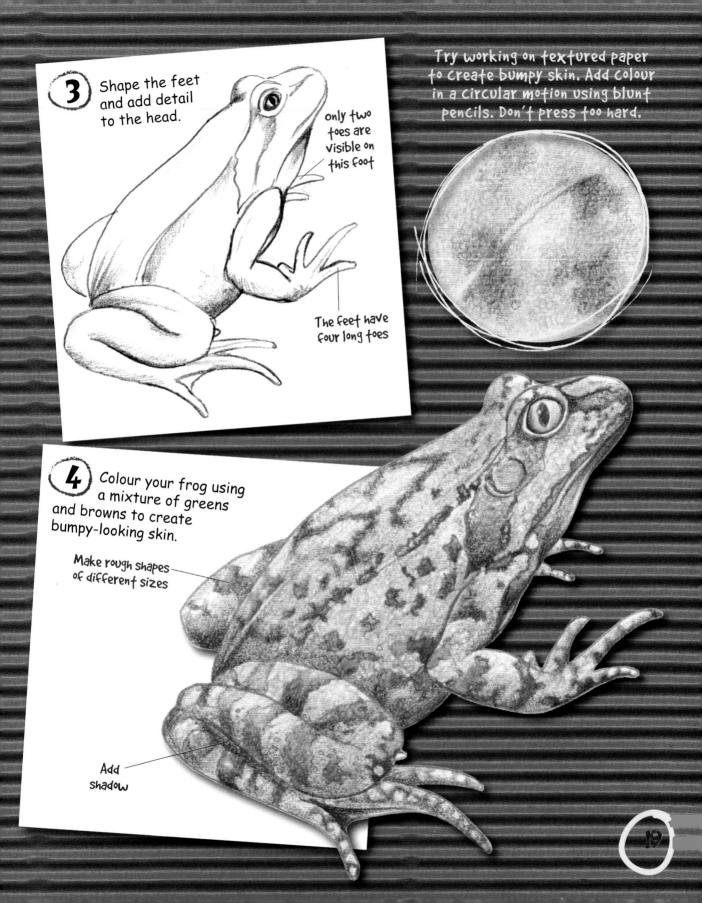

3 Shape the feet and add detail to the head.

only two toes are visible on this foot

The feet have four long toes

Try working on textured paper to create bumpy skin. Add colour in a circular motion using blunt pencils. Don't press too hard.

4 Colour your frog using a mixture of greens and browns to create bumpy-looking skin.

Make rough shapes of different sizes

Add shadow

Koala

1 Draw a large oval, with a smaller circle overlapping it at the top.

Add two small circles for ears

2 Add small eyes and the beaklike nose. Draw shapes for the arm and paw.

Little lines indicating fur

3 Add the mouth and more detail to the fur. Draw in the tree and shape the paws.

4 Shade the eyes, nose and mouth. Darken the fur around the edge of the body and head.

5 Continue shading with your regular pencil but use brown to add highlights to the fur. Use a brown crayon to create the bumpy texture of the tree.

21

shark

1 Draw the outline and fins using triangular shapes.

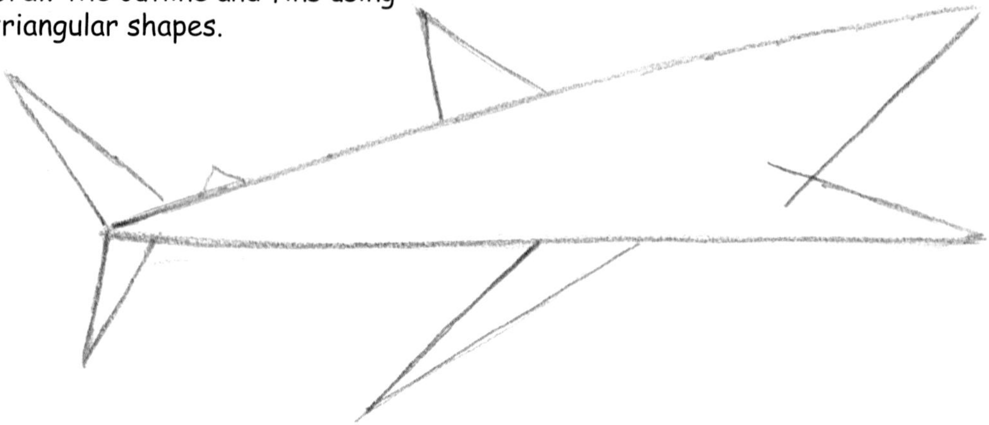

2 Soften your lines, adding shape to the fins.

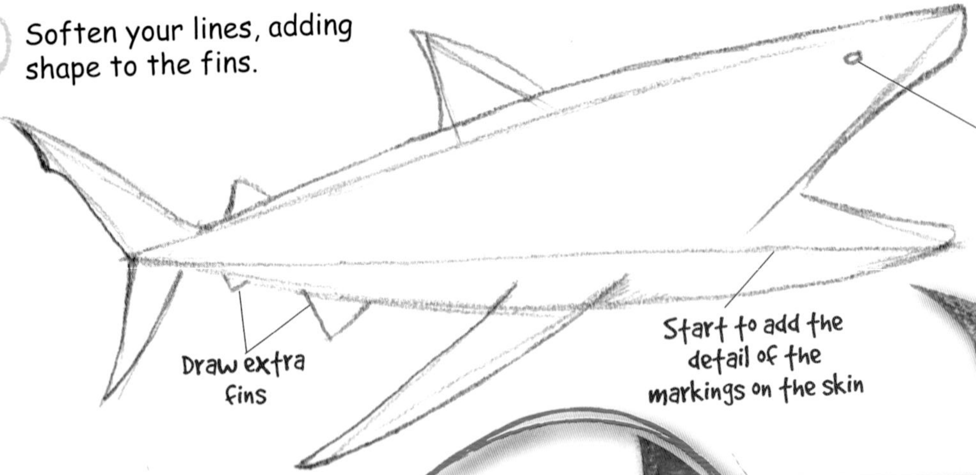

Add the eye

Draw extra fins

Start to add the detail of the markings on the skin

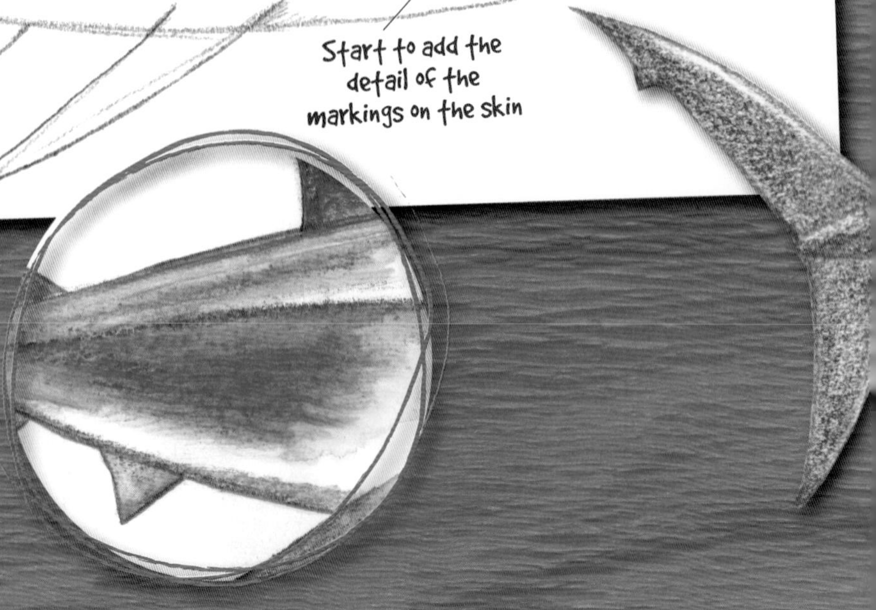

Try colouring your shark with watercolour pencil, then use a soft brush and paint over the top. When it's dry use a sharp pencil to add in the outlines.

3 Shade the body and add the gills. Draw the detail inside the mouth.

The underside is pale

4 Sharks have blue-grey backs and fins and pale underbellies. Shape the pale areas by adding areas of pale blue to shadowy places. Make the gums a pale pinky-red.

Bear

1 Draw two circles for the body and add a smaller oval for the head.

Draw straight lines for the legs

2 Shape the head, legs and paws.

Add the ears

The mouth is open

Try drawing your bear on brown paper. The paper becomes the main body colour to which you apply black and white to create shade and light.

24

3 Add more detail to the head. Begin to add the fur texture.

This eye is only just visible

Add detail to the paws

4 Shade in the eye and add the claws. Give shape to the body by adding extra detail to the fur.

5 Colour using different shades of brown and black. Don't forget the whiskers!

DOG

2 Shape the outline of the body.

Add the ears

Make the lines for the tail wavy

The back leg is bent, so add a curved line

1 Draw a big, narrow oval for the body. Add a small circle for the head and two oblong shapes for the legs and tail.

3 Erase the guidelines that you no longer need. Soften the outline to create a furry texture.

Now add the eyes, nose and mouth

Define the toes

4 Add details to the nose, ears and mouth and continue to shade the fur.

Add markings by shading parts of the head

The tail is extra fluffy

5 Pressing gently, colour your dog using lots of long lines in the direction of the fur. Add shading to the areas you have left pale with regular pencil or a brown shade.

Try working on textured paper. Use a soft pencil and colour with gentle circular movements.

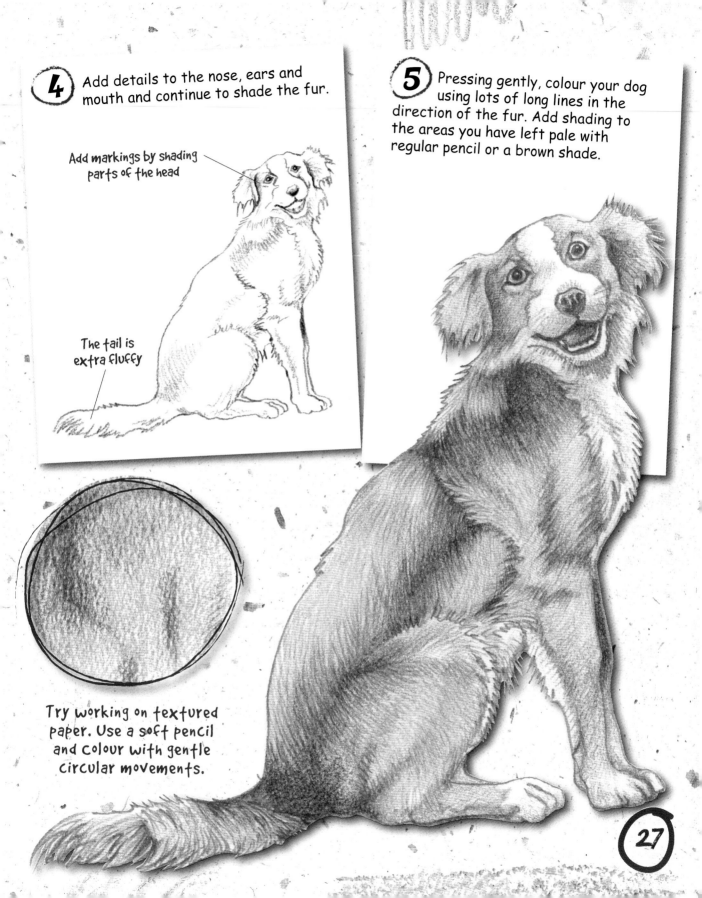

Parrot

1 Draw pointed shapes for the body, wings and tail, and a circle for the head.

Add the curve of the beak

2 Shape the beak and add a circle for the eye. Start to define the feathers on the wing and tail.

Lines for the perch

Long lines for the tail feathers

Try using watercolour pencils. Paint a little water over them to brighten the colours, and show details with a lead pencil.

Rub out the guidelines and add detail to the eye

The tip of the beak is darkest

Shape the claws

3 Shape the head and beak. Add shading to the feathers and features.

4 Colour in sections, smudging some colours together. Use black for the beak and claws.

crocodile

1 Draw a long oval for the body. Add two overlapping triangles for the head and jaws and two curved lines joining at the tip for a tail.

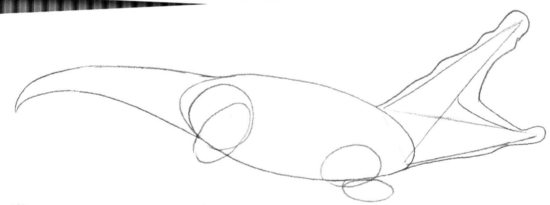

2 Shape the head and add circles for the legs and feet.

3 Add the eye and the bumpy detail of the skin. Shape the head and jaws in more detail.

Shape the front and back legs

The line of the throat is wavy

4 Finish off the legs and claws. Add detail to the head — put the teeth in now — and to the skin. Add shading to the darkest areas.

5 Define the scales with a pencil, then colour using different shades of green and brown. Use soft, circular movements and leave some areas pale to act as highlights.

The raised ridges are black

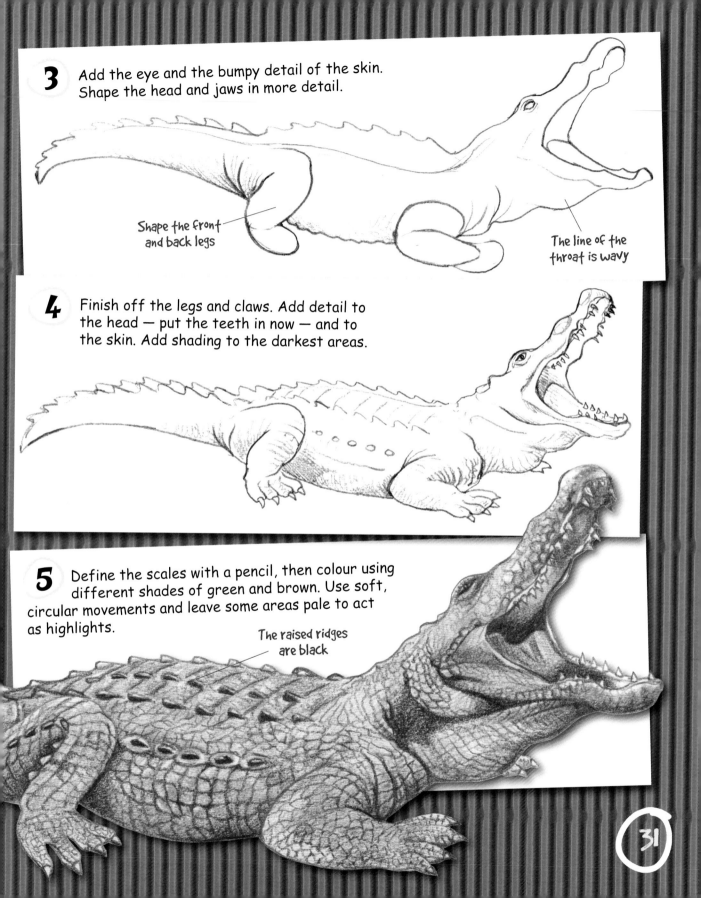

Lion

1 Draw a small oval with a larger circle around it for the head and mane. Draw a long oval for the body.

Add oblong shapes for legs

2 Add the features — don't forget the ears — and shape the legs.

Draw a guideline to help you place the features

The tail is two curved lines

3 Rub out the guide lines and add shading to the legs and belly.

Begin to shape the face

Soften the outline of the mane

finish the tail with lots of soft little lines

Define the paws

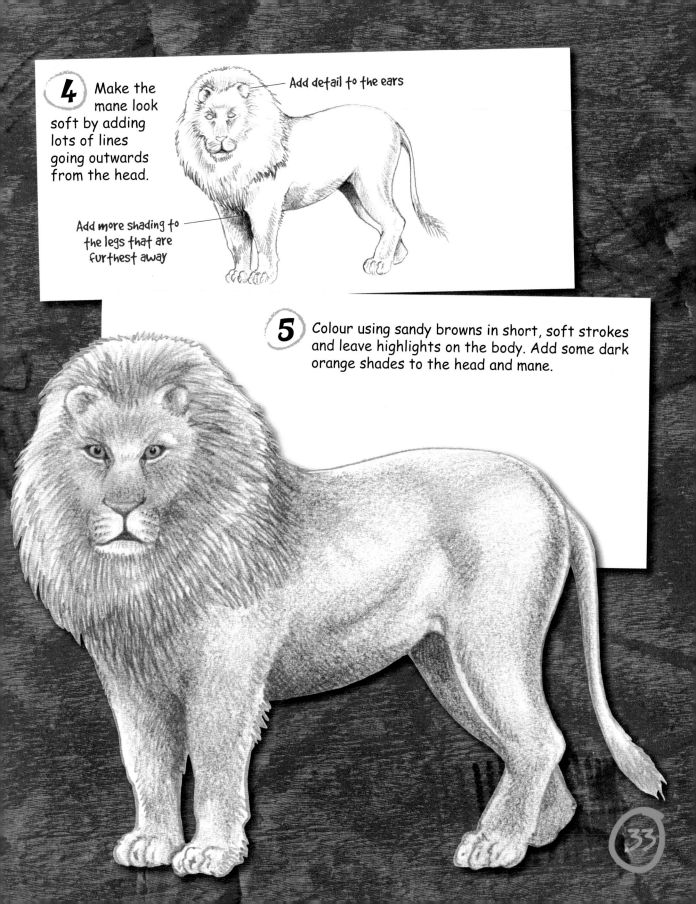

4 Make the mane look soft by adding lots of lines going outwards from the head.

Add detail to the ears

Add more shading to the legs that are furthest away

5 Colour using sandy browns in short, soft strokes and leave highlights on the body. Add some dark orange shades to the head and mane.

Giraffe

1 Draw a triangle for the head and a long shape for the neck, getting wider as it joins the body.

The body is a squashed circle

The legs are very thin triangles

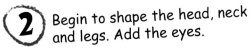

2 Begin to shape the head, neck and legs. Add the eyes.

The horns are slimmer than the ears

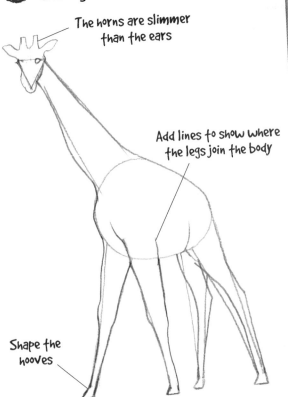

Add lines to show where the legs join the body

Shape the hooves

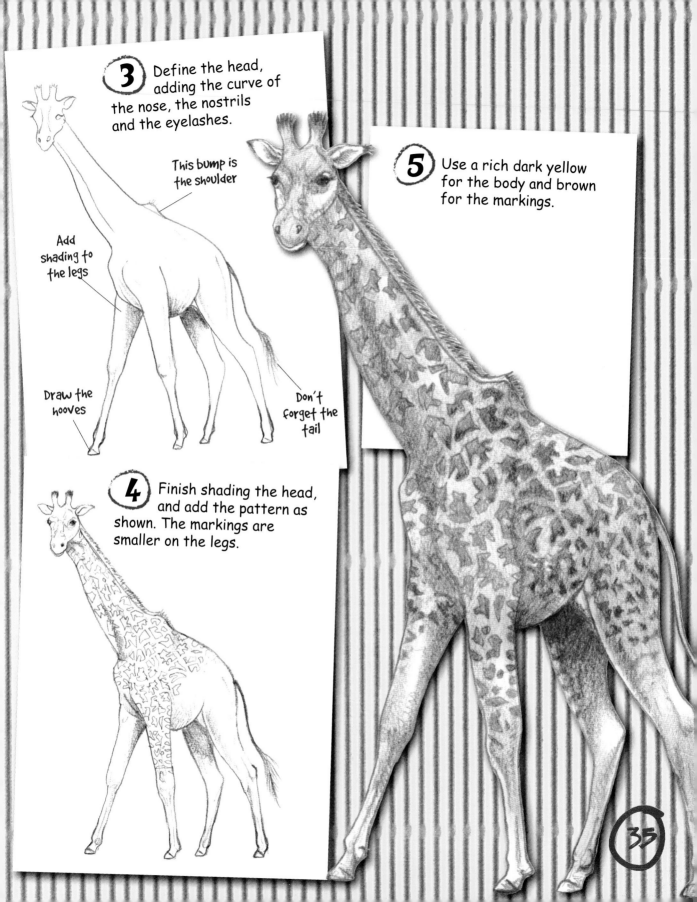

3 Define the head, adding the curve of the nose, the nostrils and the eyelashes.

This bump is the shoulder

Add shading to the legs

Draw the hooves

Don't forget the tail

4 Finish shading the head, and add the pattern as shown. The markings are smaller on the legs.

5 Use a rich dark yellow for the body and brown for the markings.

35

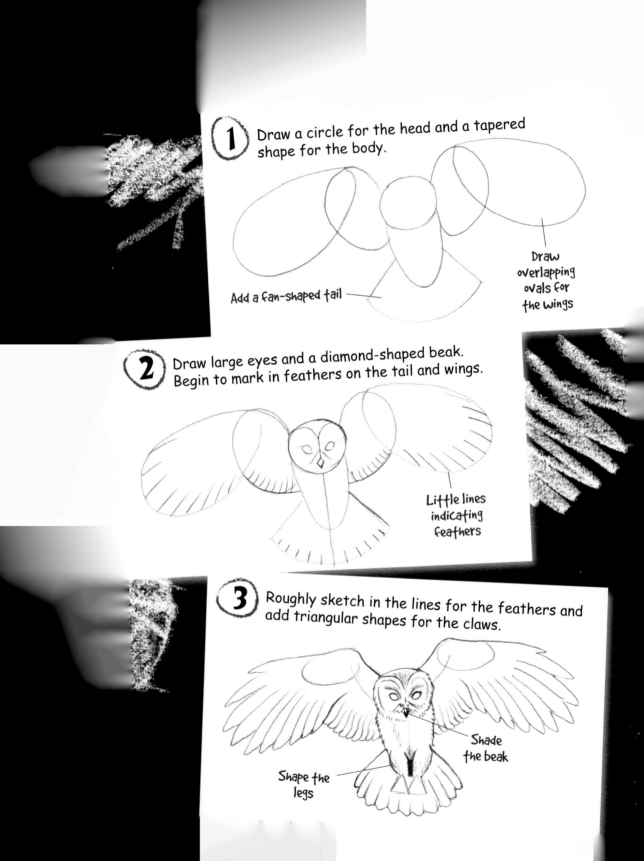

1 Draw a circle for the head and a tapered shape for the body.

Add a fan-shaped tail

Draw overlapping ovals for the wings

2 Draw large eyes and a diamond-shaped beak. Begin to mark in feathers on the tail and wings.

Little lines indicating feathers

3 Roughly sketch in the lines for the feathers and add triangular shapes for the claws.

Shade the beak

Shape the legs

4 Draw the claws and add shading to the head, body and wings.

Darken the eyes

Little lines on the body for short, soft feathers

5 Use different shades of brown to colour the feathers and add markings in black.

Try drawing your owl on black paper using a white pencil.

Elephant

1 Draw a squashed circular body and a rough, pointed triangle for the head and trunk. Draw slim rectangles for legs.

Add an oval for the ear

2 Shape the head and body. Flatten the line of the bottom of the ear.

The body is angular

The trunk is two curving lines

Shape the legs

3 Shape the edge of the ear and add the eye. Add shading to the belly and legs.

Add the tail

4 To add texture to the skin, add long horizontal lines, especially on the trunk and legs. Define the creases in the ear.

Add the tusks

Draw circles for toenails

5 Add colour with a grey pencil, using a light brown for highlights. Leave the tusks pale with a little brown shading.

Horse

1 Draw an oval for the body and triangles for the head, neck and legs.

2 Begin to shape the head, neck and body. Add the eye and ears.

curve the line of the back

3 Add the mane and flowing tail. Shape the hooves. Erase all the guidelines.

Add a line for the mouth

Begin to add shading

Shape the legs

Try using a blunt pencil to get an even colour for the body. Then sharpen the pencil and use it to add fine lines of hair.

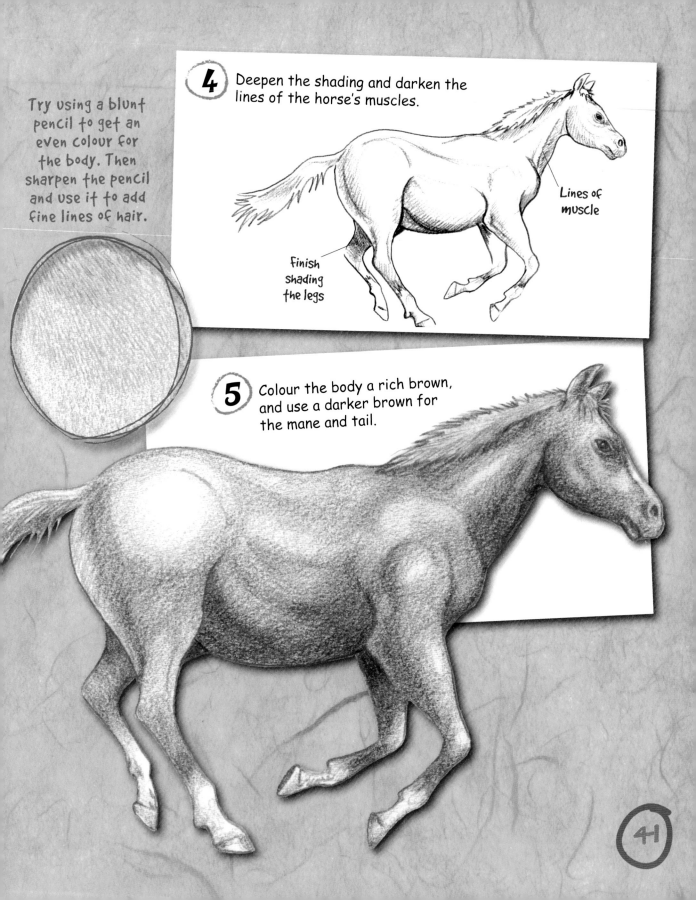

4 Deepen the shading and darken the lines of the horse's muscles.

Lines of muscle

Finish shading the legs

5 Colour the body a rich brown, and use a darker brown for the mane and tail.

cat

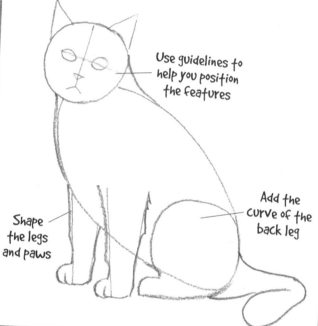

2 Draw circles for eyes and a triangle for the nose. The mouth is two lines. Add the tail.

Use guidelines to help you position the features

Add the curve of the back leg

Shape the legs and paws

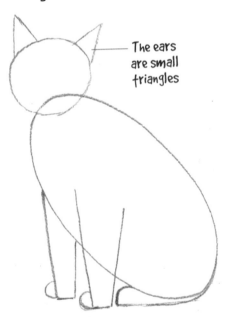

1 Draw a slanted oval for the body and a circle for a head. Add straight lines for the legs.

The ears are small triangles

Try drawing fur on grey paper using a darker grey and white for highlights. Use black for stripes, and blend with the other colours.

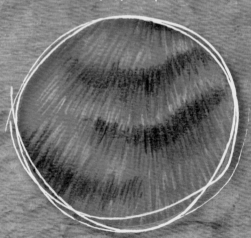

3 Soften the outline and begin to add shading. Erase the guidelines.

Begin to add markings around the eyes

4 Make the features more detailed. Continue to add texture to the fur.

Soften the head, adding lots of little lines

5 Colour using shades of grey in short lines, leaving patches on the chest and legs pale. Draw fine lines for the whiskers. Add stripes of different thickness in black. Colour the eyes amber.

Gallery

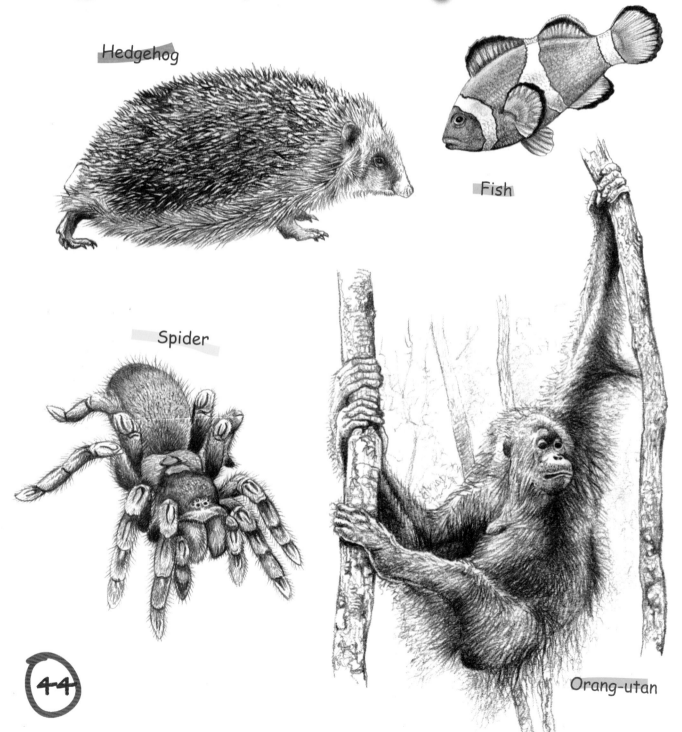

Hedgehog

Fish

Spider

Orang-utan

Panda

Horse

Toucan

Lizard

Reptiles often have markings in vertical lines down their bodies

45

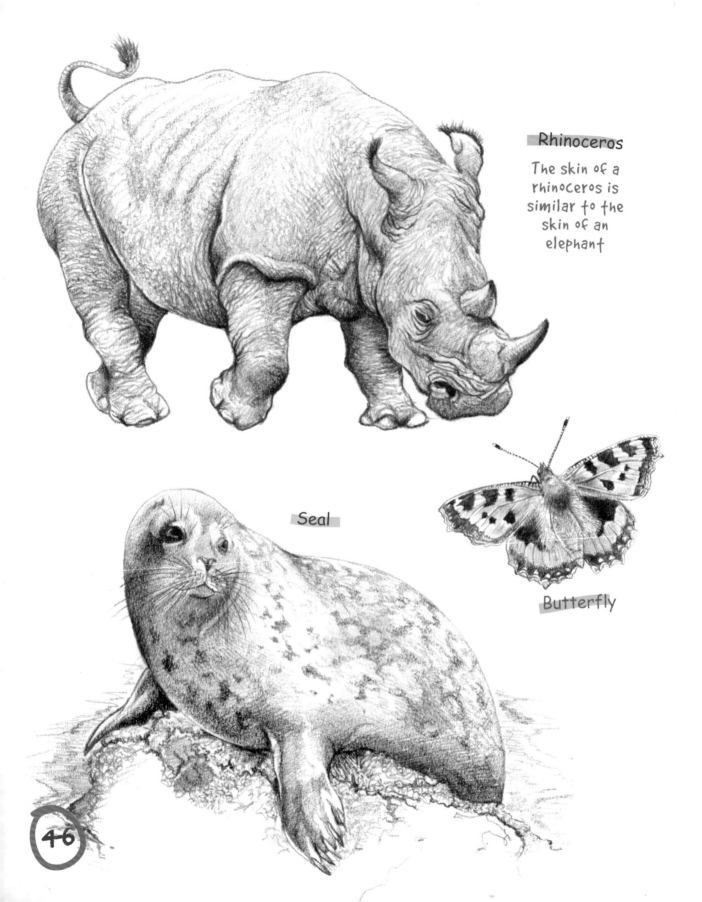

Rhinoceros

The skin of a rhinoceros is similar to the skin of an elephant

Seal

Butterfly

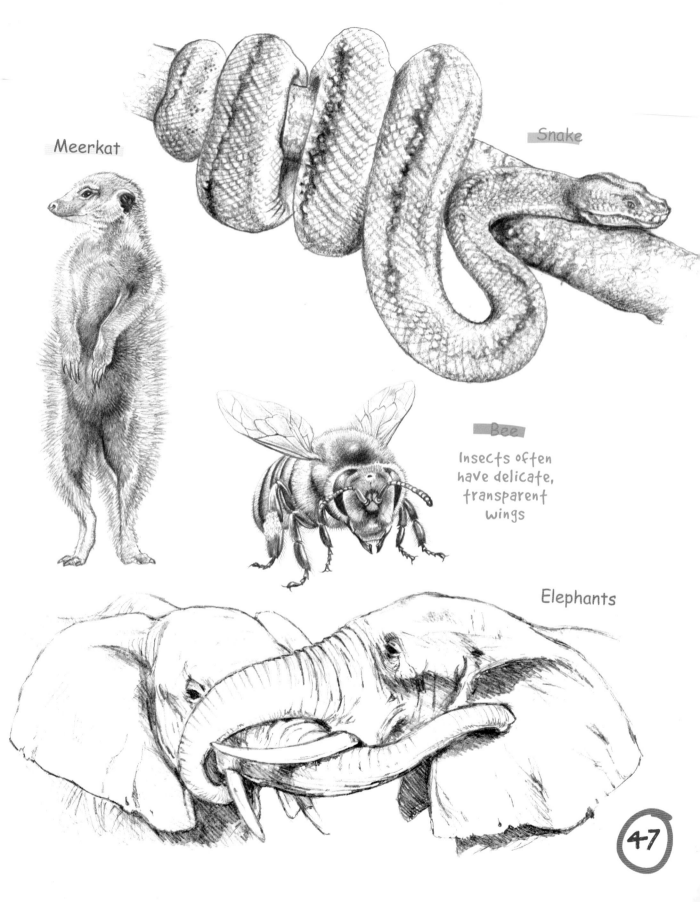

Meerkat

Snake

Bee

Insects often have delicate, transparent wings

Elephants

47

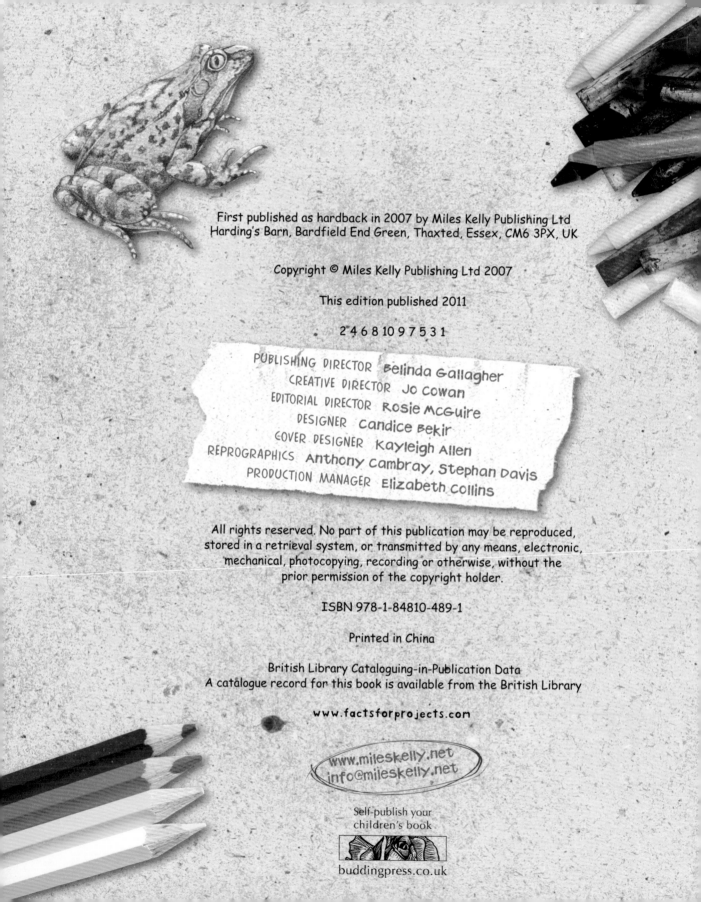

First published as hardback in 2007 by Miles Kelly Publishing Ltd
Harding's Barn, Bardfield End Green, Thaxted, Essex, CM6 3PX, UK

Copyright © Miles Kelly Publishing Ltd 2007

This edition published 2011

2 4 6 8 10 9 7 5 3 1

PUBLISHING DIRECTOR Belinda Gallagher
CREATIVE DIRECTOR Jo Cowan
EDITORIAL DIRECTOR Rosie McGuire
DESIGNER Candice Bekir
COVER DESIGNER Kayleigh Allen
REPROGRAPHICS Anthony Cambray, Stephan Davis
PRODUCTION MANAGER Elizabeth Collins

ISBN 978-1-84810-489-1

Printed in China

British Library Cataloguing-in-Publication Data
A catalogue record for this book is available from the British Library

www.factsforprojects.com

www.mileskelly.net
info@mileskelly.net

Self-publish your
children's book

buddingpress.co.uk